HANDS-ON
JOBS

CONSTRUCTION
WORKERS

ELIZABETH MORGAN

PowerKiDS
press™

New York

Published in 2016 by The Rosen Publishing Group, Inc.
29 East 21st Street, New York, NY 10010

First Edition

Editor: Katie Kawa
Book Design: Reann Nye

Photo Credits: Cover Ron Levine/The Image Bank/Getty Images; cover, pp. 3–24 (background texture) Toluk/Shutterstock.com; p. 5 Hero Images/Getty Images; p. 6 ruigsantos/Shutterstock.com; p. 7 https://commons.wikimedia.org/wiki/File:Old_timer_structural_worker2.jpg; p. 9 Goodluz/Shutterstock.com; p. 11 ndoeljindoel/Shutterstock.com; p. 13 maradonna 8888/Shutterstock.com; p. 15 serato/Shutterstock.com; p. 17 (drill) Dinga/Shutterstock.com; p. 17 (saw) MNI/Shutterstock.com; p. 17 (nail gun) Photoexpert/Shutterstock.com; p. 17 (jackhammer) stefan11/Shutterstock.com; p. 17 (pliers) LU YAO/Shutterstock.com; p. 17 (excavator) maggee/Shutterstock.com; p. 17 (background) alexmillos/Shutterstock.com; p. 18 Francesco R. Iacomino/Shutterstock.com; p. 19 Hybrid Images/Cultura/Getty Images; p. 21 stevecoleimages/E+/Getty Images; p. 22 Ron Levine/Photographer's Choice/Getty Images.

Library of Congress Cataloging-in-Publication Data

Morgan, Elizabeth, author.
Construction workers / Elizabeth Morgan.
    pages cm. — (Hands-on jobs)
Includes index.
ISBN 978-1-5081-4355-0 (pbk.)
ISBN 978-1-5081-4356-7 (6 pack)
ISBN 978-1-5081-4357-4 (library binding)
1. Building—Vocational guidance—Juvenile literature. 2. Construction workers—Juvenile literature. I. Title.
TH159.M67 2016
690.023—dc23

2015023459

Manufactured in the United States of America

CPSIA Compliance Information: Batch #BW16PK: For Further Information contact Rosen Publishing, New York, New York at 1-800-237-9932

3 6830 00114 5869

CONTENTS

BUILD IT!

It takes a lot of hard work to construct the roads and buildings we see around us every day. Construction workers build everything from skyscrapers and schools to houses and highways.

Construction workers learn to use many different tools to do their job and stay safe while they work. They also learn to operate big machines, such as cranes and dump trucks, in order to move heavy things around their work area. If you enjoy working with tools and building things, this could be a good job for you. It's not an easy job, but it's an important one!

DIGGING DEEPER

Construction workers often wear bright vests while they're at work. This makes it easier for them to be seen, which helps them avoid getting hurt.

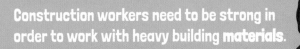

Construction workers need to be strong in order to work with heavy building **materials**.

AN IMPORTANT CAREER

Construction workers have chosen a very important career. They build and repair the houses we live in, the roads we drive on, and famous buildings around the world.

Construction workers do many different things around a construction site, which is the area where something is being built. First, they need to make sure the site is clear for building by removing **debris** that could get in the way. Then, they help unload the materials that are needed for building, such as lumber or steel beams. After the site is ready, construction workers can begin to build.

DIGGING DEEPER

Between 1930 and 1931, around 3,000 construction workers built the Empire State Building, which is one of the tallest and most famous buildings in New York City.

Shown here is a construction worker doing his part to build the famous Empire State Building. The amazing skyscrapers in big cities are the result of the hard work of thousands of construction workers.

LEARNING ON THE JOB

Construction workers learn how to do their job in different ways. Some go to schools called trade schools or vocational schools to learn to be construction workers. Others learn through on-the-job training with help from workers with more **experience**.

Some construction workers are trained through apprenticeship programs. These programs combine **technical instruction** and on-the-job training. Apprentices learn the basic skills necessary to work in all areas of construction. They also learn how to stay safe and avoid getting hurt on the job. A person who's interested in being part of a construction apprenticeship program should be at least 18 years old.

If you want to become a construction worker, you have to be ready to learn from other workers with more experience. They know better than anyone else how to do their job well and stay safe while doing it.

DIGGING DEEPER

Some construction workers go through special training in order to be **certified** to remove hazardous, or unsafe, materials from construction sites. Certified construction workers have proven they know how to do the hardest and most **dangerous** jobs on construction sites.

SPECIAL SKILLS

Construction workers often learn skills on the job, but it's helpful for them to already have certain skills in order to be successful. Physical strength is important because construction workers lift heavy things very often. Construction workers also need physical **stamina** because they often work long hours in hot or cold weather doing tasks that are hard on their body.

Strong math skills are also important because construction workers do a lot of measuring. In addition, construction workers should know how to use basic tools and how to work with different building materials.

DIGGING DEEPER

Construction workers often work high above the ground when building skyscrapers. These men and women can't have a fear of heights!

Strong reading skills are important for some construction workers because they need to read blueprints. A blueprint is a building plan.

BUILDING CONSTRUCTION

Different kinds of construction jobs call for workers with different kinds of training and skills. Building construction is a branch of construction work that includes projects such as houses, huge office buildings, and shopping centers.

Concrete is one of the most common materials used in building construction. It's a mixture of water, powdered **cement**, and either gravel or sand. Construction workers pour the concrete. Then, they make sure it's smooth, so it dries evenly. Concrete is strong and hard once it dries. Often, steel is put in the concrete to make it stronger. This is called reinforced concrete.

DIGGING DEEPER

Construction workers began using steel to support **structures** in the 1800s. The discovery that steel could be used to create a building's frame led to the construction of the first skyscrapers.

Steel beams form the frame of most of today's tallest buildings. Construction workers make sure those beams are in the right place.

ON THE ROAD

Road construction is another major area of construction work. All the roads we drive on—including the highways that connect cities and states—were created by construction workers.

In order to build a road, construction workers clear the chosen land and dig into the earth to create an embankment, or raised area of dirt. The construction workers then create a strong road **foundation** with dirt and gravel. Then, they pave the road with concrete or asphalt, which is also known as blacktop. Construction workers also paint the yellow and white lines we see on roads across the country.

DIGGING DEEPER

Construction workers who build or repair roads often work through the night in order to avoid disrupting traffic. Bright lights are placed around these roads to help the construction workers see in the dark.

Construction workers build roads, and they also repair them. They fill potholes and fix bumps to make the road surface smoother for drivers.

TOOLS OF THE TRADE

Whether construction workers are building roads, buildings, bridges, or other structures, they need to use many different kinds of tools. Some tools are simple, such as hammers and screwdrivers. Construction workers also use power tools, such as drills and circular saws.

Some construction workers are trained to operate the big machines used to lift and carry heavy materials. These construction workers might operate the cranes that carry steel beams to the top of tall building projects. Some operate bulldozers. A bulldozer is a tractor used on construction sites that has a big blade to push dirt, sand, or debris.

DIGGING DEEPER

Construction workers often need to be certified before they can use the biggest machines on construction sites, such as cranes. They go through special training to prove they can operate these dangerous machines safely.

COMMON CONSTRUCTION TOOLS

PLIERS
bend and cut wire;
hold small objects

DRILL
makes holes in
hard material

SAW
cuts into hard material
(wood, metal)

NAIL GUN
drives nails into wood
or other hard material

JACKHAMMER
breaks hard substances,
such as concrete,
into pieces

EXCAVATOR
moves and removes
earth and debris from
a construction site

This chart shows some common tools used by construction workers. Some of these tools, such as pliers, are simple machines. Others, such as excavators, are **complex** machines.

17

STAYING SAFE

Working on a construction site can be very rewarding. You get to build amazing buildings, roads, and other structures using your hands and helpful tools. However, it can also be dangerous. Construction workers have a high chance of getting hurt because they work with heavy materials and powerful machines.

In order to stay safe at work, construction workers wear a helmet, which is also known as a hard hat. They also wear safety goggles over their eyes to keep them safe from flying debris. Special gloves keep their hands from getting cut or burned.

DIGGING DEEPER

Construction workers generally wear steel-toe boots to keep their feet safe from falling objects.

Safety gear helps construction workers do their job without worrying about getting hurt.

FIRST CONSTRUCTION PROJECTS

Do you think being a construction worker sounds like a good job for you? It's never too early to start working on small construction projects of your own. These projects will help you learn about the tools you'll use and the skills you'll need if you become a construction worker when you grow up.

One fun construction project is building a birdhouse for your backyard. After that, you could build a tree house to play in! Always ask an adult to help you whenever you start a new construction project, especially if you're going to be using tools such as a hammer or a saw.

DIGGING DEEPER

Some schools offer classes that teach skills used by construction workers. Taking one of these classes could help you prepare for a career as a construction worker.

Building a birdhouse helps you practice many of the skills used by construction workers. It also shows you how much fun it is to build something with your own hands.

HELPING THEIR COMMUNITY

Construction workers are an important part of all communities. You can often see them at work around your city or town. The people who've chosen this job aren't afraid to work high above the ground, lift heavy objects, and get their hands dirty.

Some construction workers go on to lead their own crews of workers. They're called construction foremen. If you want to be a construction worker or a foreman someday, you can start learning the skills you'll need now. Find a building project you can do with an adult's help, and have fun trying out this hands-on job!

GLOSSARY

cement: A soft gray powder mixed with water and other substances to make concrete.

certify: To officially say that someone has met certain standards or requirements.

complex: Having many parts.

dangerous: Not safe.

debris: Broken pieces of objects or objects left somewhere because they are not wanted.

experience: The length of time someone has been doing an activity or job.

foundation: The lowest part of a structure that supports the structure.

material: Something from which something else can be made.

stamina: Strength that allows a person to keep doing something for a long time.

structure: A building or other object that is constructed.

technical instruction: The teaching of a particular subject, especially how machines work or how a particular kind of work is done.

INDEX

WEBSITES

Due to the changing nature of Internet links, PowerKids Press has developed an online list of websites related to the subject of this book. This site is updated regularly. Please use this link to access the list: www.powerkidslinks.com/hoj/conwk